SIGMA MALE MASTERY

Thriving in a World

Of

Alphas and Betas

By

HARRY POOL

Contents

Introduction: Unveiling the Sigma Male 1

Understanding the Sigma Male: A Deep Dive into the Enigmatic Personality 6

Alpha, Beta, and Sigma: Unraveling the Complexities of Male Archetypes 12

The Complex Psyche of Sigma Males: Unraveling the Enigma 19

The Sigma Male's Approach to Relationships: Navigating the Path of Independence and Connection 25

Success and Achievement Strategies for Sigma Males: Thriving on Their Own Terms 30

The Art of Independence: Nurturing the Sigma Male's Self-Reliance 35

Mastering the Art of Social Skills and Effective Communication: A Guide to Thriving in a Diverse World 40

Embracing Silence and Solitude: The Sigma Male's Path to Inner Strength 47

Navigating the Sigma Male Journey: Challenges and Misconceptions Unveiled 54

Sigma Male Role Models: Defying Conventions and Shaping the World 61

Embarking on the Journey of Self-Discovery and Personal Growth: Unleash Your Potential................71

The Future of Sigma Males: Navigating the Changing Landscape 78

The Sigma Male's Guide to Leadership and Influence: Navigating the Path Less Traveled 84

Navigating the Sigma Male Lifestyle: Challenges and Rewards................90

Sigma Males and Society's Expectations: Breaking Stereotypes 96

Sigma Male Archetypes in Pop Culture: Unmasking the Nonconformists 101

Sigma Males and Personal Fulfillment: Finding Your Path................106

Conclusion: Embracing the Sigma Male Lifestyle 112

Introduction: Unveiling the Sigma Male

In a world where personality archetypes are often distilled into categories like Alpha and Beta, there exists a less explored, enigmatic figure - the Sigma male. This introduction aims to peel back the layers of mystery surrounding this unique personality type, setting the stage for an exploration into the realm of Sigma males. Through the pages of this book, we will embark on a journey to understand who Sigma males are, how they navigate the complex social landscape, and the keys to their success and fulfillment.

Defining the Sigma Male

The Sigma male, like the Alpha and Beta, is a conceptual archetype used to describe certain traits, behaviors, and attitudes often observed in individuals. However, unlike Alphas who are seen as dominant and assertive or Betas who tend to be more passive and conforming, Sigma males defy easy categorization. They are often characterized by a sense of independence, self-reliance, and an unconventional approach to life.

At this point, it's crucial to clarify that Sigma males are not an inherently superior or inferior personality type compared to Alphas or Betas. Instead, they represent a unique and valuable facet of human diversity. Sigma males possess their own strengths and weaknesses, and understanding their characteristics can shed light on the rich tapestry of human personalities.

The Mystery of Sigma Males

The Sigma male, in many ways, embodies the mystery and intrigue often associated with figures who defy societal norms and expectations. They are the silent observers in the room, the individuals who seem to march to the beat of their own drum, often eluding easy comprehension. The mystery lies not in their complexity but in their divergence from the well-trodden paths laid out by society.

In popular culture and social circles, Sigma males have been the subject of fascination and curiosity. They are the characters who quietly steal the spotlight in literature, film, and real life. But what exactly makes them tick? What drives their choices, actions, and worldviews? These are the questions that we will attempt to unravel in the pages ahead.

The Purpose of This Book

The purpose of this book is twofold. First, it aims to provide a comprehensive understanding of Sigma males, delving deep into their psyche, behaviors, and social dynamics. By the end of this journey, you, the reader, will have a clearer grasp of what it means to be a Sigma male and how they interact with the world around them.

Second, and perhaps more importantly, this book seeks to offer practical insights and guidance. Whether you identify as a Sigma male yourself, know someone who does, or simply want to expand your knowledge of human personalities, this book will equip you with the tools to thrive in a world filled with Alphas and Betas. It's a guide for Sigma males seeking to harness their unique qualities for personal and professional success, as well as for those interested in building meaningful connections with Sigma males.

What You Can Expect to Learn

As you journey through the chapters of this book, you can expect to gain a profound understanding of:

1. ***The Sigma Male Blueprint:*** We will dissect the core characteristics and traits that define Sigma males, painting a vivid picture of their mindset and behavior.

2. ***Sigma Male Psychology:*** Dive into the inner workings of Sigma males' minds, exploring the factors that shape their identity and choices.

3. ***Social Dynamics:*** Understand how Sigma males navigate relationships, both romantic and platonic, and how they interact with Alphas and Betas.

4. ***Success and Achievement:*** Discover the unique strategies Sigma males employ to set and

accomplish their goals, often in unconventional ways.

5. **Self-Improvement:** Find practical tips and advice for Sigma males looking to enhance their social skills, self-confidence, and personal growth.

6. **Challenges and Misconceptions:** Address common misconceptions and challenges that Sigma males encounter, along with strategies for overcoming them.

7. **Role Models:** Meet real-life Sigma male figures who have excelled in various fields, drawing inspiration from their stories.

8. **The Future of Sigma Males:** Speculate on how the role of Sigma males may evolve in the ever-changing landscape of society.

This book is not just a passive read; it's an invitation to introspection, a guide for personal growth, and a source of empowerment. Whether you are a Sigma male charting your path or an inquisitive reader eager to explore the complexities of human personality, you'll find valuable insights and knowledge within these pages.

In closing, the journey into the world of Sigma males is one of intrigue and discovery. Prepare to embark on a quest to unveil the enigma, embrace the nuances, and master the art of thriving as a Sigma male in a world that often expects conformity. It's time to lift the veil and embark on this transformative journey together.

Understanding the Sigma Male: A Deep Dive into the Enigmatic Personality

In the realm of human personality archetypes, the Sigma male stands as an intriguing and somewhat elusive figure. To truly understand what it means to be a Sigma male, we must embark on a journey through their distinctive characteristics, behaviors, and the complex interplay of history and culture that has given rise to this archetype.

Defining Sigma Males: Beyond Alpha and Beta

At its core, the Sigma male represents a distinct personality type that deviates from the conventional Alpha and Beta male archetypes. While Alphas are often seen as assertive leaders and Betas as more passive followers, Sigma males chart their own course, often characterized by the following traits:

1. **Independence:** Sigma males value their autonomy and self-sufficiency. They are not driven by a need for social validation or conformity to societal norms. Instead, they follow their instincts and intuition.

2. **Self-Reliance:** These individuals have a knack for self-reliance. They are resourceful problem solvers who prefer to rely on their skills and

knowledge rather than seeking external assistance.

3. **Introversion:** Sigma males tend to be introverted, finding strength and comfort in solitude. They use their alone time for self-reflection and personal growth.

4. **Observational Skills:** They are keen observers of their environment, often possessing a heightened sense of awareness. This ability enables them to read situations and people effectively.

5. **Silent Confidence:** Unlike the overt confidence associated with Alphas, Sigma males exhibit a quieter, understated confidence that can be equally compelling.

6. **Nonconformity:** Sigma males resist conformity and often challenge the status quo. They are not easily swayed by societal expectations.

7. **Selective Socialization:** While they may not be social butterflies, Sigma males form deep and meaningful connections with a select few individuals. Quality over quantity is their mantra when it comes to relationships.

Historical Roots of the Sigma Male

The Sigma male archetype did not emerge overnight; rather, it has deep historical roots that can be traced through various cultures and time periods. To understand the Sigma male fully, it is essential to consider the historical context that has shaped their identity.

1. **Ancient Philosophers and Thinkers:** In ancient Greece, philosophers like Diogenes and Heraclitus displayed traits that align with the Sigma male archetype. Diogenes, known for his ascetic lifestyle and disregard for social norms, particularly embodies the spirit of independence and nonconformity.

2. **Frontiersmen and Explorers:** Throughout history, individuals who ventured into uncharted territories, such as frontiersmen and explorers, displayed Sigma male qualities. Their self-reliance, resilience, and determination were essential for survival in unknown lands.

3. **Literary and Cultural Figures:** Literary characters like Sherlock Holmes and cultural figures such as Clint Eastwood's "Man with No Name" character in spaghetti westerns exemplify Sigma male traits. These characters are often portrayed as self-reliant, independent, and enigmatic.

4. **Historical Outliers:** In various historical contexts, outliers who deviated from societal norms and expectations displayed Sigma male

characteristics. These individuals often challenged existing power structures and norms.

5. **Modern Context:** In contemporary times, Sigma males continue to emerge in various fields. They are often found among entrepreneurs, artists, and thinkers who chart their paths, often in unconventional ways.

Cultural and Media Portrayals

The cultural and media representations of Sigma males have both reflected and influenced the perception of this archetype. These portrayals have contributed to the mystique surrounding Sigma males:

1. **Literature and Film:** Characters like James Bond, a suave and independent secret agent, embody Sigma male qualities. Similarly, antiheroes in literature and film often possess Sigma traits.

2. **Anti-Establishment Movements:** In the counterculture movements of the 1960s and 1970s, many activists exhibited Sigma male characteristics. They rejected traditional authority and sought social change on their terms.

3. **Entrepreneurship:** In the world of business, entrepreneurs who break away from corporate structures to create their ventures often exhibit

Sigma qualities. They are driven by a desire for independence and innovation.

4. **Online Communities:** The rise of the internet has allowed Sigma males to connect and share their experiences in online communities. These platforms have provided a space for self-identifying Sigma males to discuss their perspectives and challenges.

Sigma Male or Stereotype?

It's essential to acknowledge that the concept of Sigma males has also faced criticism and skepticism. Some argue that it is an oversimplified stereotype that doesn't accurately capture the complexity of human personality. Others view it as a romanticized idealization of introverted and independent individuals.

While it is true that no archetype can fully encapsulate the diversity of human personalities, the Sigma male concept serves as a useful framework for understanding a particular set of traits and behaviors. It is a starting point for exploring the variations within this personality type and understanding how Sigma males interact with the world.

The Sigma Male Continuum

It's crucial to recognize that the Sigma male archetype exists on a continuum. Not all Sigma males exhibit every characteristic to the same degree. Some may lean more toward introversion, while others emphasize independence or self-reliance. Individuals may also evolve and change over time, adopting different traits and behaviors based on life experiences and personal growth.

Understanding the Sigma male, therefore, involves appreciating the complexity and individuality of each person who identifies with this archetype. While there are common threads that connect Sigma males, no two are precisely alike.

In the chapters that follow, we will delve deeper into the psychology, social dynamics, challenges, and successes of Sigma males. By the end of this exploration, you will have a well-rounded understanding of this multifaceted personality type, shedding light on their enigmatic nature and offering practical insights for thriving as a Sigma male or connecting with them in your personal and professional life.

Alpha, Beta, and Sigma: Unraveling the Complexities of Male Archetypes

In the intricate tapestry of male personalities, the Alpha, Beta, and Sigma archetypes form distinct threads, each contributing to the rich diversity of human behavior. To navigate the intricate interplay of these archetypes effectively, it is crucial to analyze their differences, highlight their respective strengths and weaknesses, and understand how they shape individuals' lives and interactions.

Defining the Archetypes: Alpha, Beta, and Sigma

Before delving into the comparisons and contrasts, let's establish a clear understanding of each archetype:

1. **Alpha Males:** Alpha males are often portrayed as dominant, assertive, and confident individuals. They thrive in leadership roles, are charismatic, and tend to command attention in social and professional settings. Alphas are stereotypically seen as the leaders of the pack, driven by ambition and a desire for power and influence.

2. **Beta Males:** Beta males are typically considered more passive, accommodating, and less assertive than Alphas. They often prioritize stability, cooperation, and maintaining harmonious relationships. Beta males may be seen as

followers rather than leaders, and they value security and social integration.

3. **Sigma Males:** Sigma males, in contrast to Alphas and Betas, are characterized by their independence, self-reliance, and nonconformity. They do not seek to dominate social hierarchies or conform to societal norms. Instead, they chart their paths, often operating on the fringes of established structures.

Comparing and Contrasting the Archetypes

To gain a comprehensive understanding of these archetypes, it's essential to explore their key differences and similarities:

1. Social Dominance:

- **Alpha:** Alphas seek social dominance and often thrive in leadership positions. They are comfortable in the spotlight and have a knack for influencing others.

- **Beta:** Betas typically do not seek social dominance and are more content in supporting roles. They value cooperation and often prefer to follow the lead of Alphas or others.

- **Sigma:** Sigmas, by nature, are not interested in social dominance. They value independence and self-reliance over leading or following. They may display dominance in specific situations but do not seek it as a primary goal.

2. Social Interaction:

- ***Alpha:*** Alphas are highly skilled in social interaction and often excel at networking and making connections. They are assertive and confident communicators.

- ***Beta:*** Betas are adept at forming and maintaining relationships. They value harmony and are generally skilled at resolving conflicts and fostering connections.

- ***Sigma:*** Sigmas are typically introverted and may find social interactions draining. They prioritize quality over quantity in their relationships and often have a smaller, close-knit social circle.

3. Ambition and Goals:

- ***Alpha:*** Alphas are ambitious and driven by a desire for power, success, and recognition. They are goal-oriented and are often willing to take risks to achieve their objectives.

- ***Beta:*** Betas tend to be more risk-averse and prioritize stability and security. They may have ambitions but often approach them cautiously.

- ***Sigma:*** Sigmas pursue their goals independently and on their terms. They are not motivated by societal recognition or conformity but by personal fulfillment and self-determination.

4. *Conformity to Social Norms:*

- ***Alpha:*** Alphas may conform to social norms when it aligns with their goals and image. However, they are also willing to challenge norms when necessary.

- ***Beta:*** Betas often conform to social norms and seek to fit into established structures. They value societal acceptance and may be less inclined to challenge norms.

- ***Sigma:*** Sigmas actively resist conformity to societal norms. They prefer to operate outside the confines of established structures and chart their paths.

5. *Strengths and Weaknesses of Each Archetype*

Understanding the strengths and weaknesses of each archetype can shed light on their dynamics in various contexts:

Alpha:

Strengths:

- Leadership skills and charisma.

- Confidence and assertiveness.

- Willingness to take risks.
- Ability to influence and inspire others.

Weaknesses:

- Can be overly dominant or aggressive.
- May struggle with empathy or cooperation.
- Risk of burnout due to high ambition and pressure.

Beta:

Strengths:

- Strong interpersonal skills and empathy.
- Ability to maintain harmony in relationships.
- Risk-averse nature leads to stability.
- Cooperative and team-oriented.

Weaknesses:

- May struggle with assertiveness.
- Tendency to avoid conflict, which can lead to bottling up emotions.
- May miss out on opportunities due to risk aversion.

Sigma:

Strengths:

- Independence and self-reliance.
- Ability to think critically and chart unconventional paths.
- Resilience in the face of societal pressure.
- Authenticity and nonconformity.

Weaknesses:

- Difficulty in forming and maintaining relationships.
- Potential for isolation due to introverted tendencies.
- Resistance to societal norms may lead to conflicts.

Interplay and Fluidity of Archetypes

It's important to note that individuals often exhibit a blend of these archetypal traits rather than fitting neatly into one category. Human personality is complex and multifaceted, and one's behavior may vary depending on context, life experiences, and personal growth.

Furthermore, individuals may evolve and adapt their behavior over time, transitioning between archetypes or adopting qualities from each as circumstances dictate. For instance, a Sigma male may develop Alpha traits in a professional setting, while a Beta male may exhibit Sigma qualities when pursuing a personal passion.

The Value of Understanding Archetypes

Understanding these archetypes offers valuable insights into human behavior and interpersonal dynamics. It allows individuals to:

- Gain self-awareness and better understand their own tendencies and motivations.

- Improve communication and relationships by recognizing the traits and preferences of others.

- Navigate social and professional situations with greater clarity and adaptability.

- Foster empathy and acceptance by appreciating the diversity of personality types.

In conclusion, the Alpha, Beta, and Sigma archetypes represent distinct facets of male personality, each with its strengths and weaknesses. While these archetypes provide a framework for understanding behavior, it's essential to remember that individuals are not confined to a single archetype but possess the flexibility to adapt and evolve as they navigate the complexities of life.

The Complex Psyche of Sigma Males: Unraveling the Enigma

The Sigma male, characterized by independence, self-reliance, and a nonconformist nature, possesses a unique psychological profile that distinguishes them from other personality types. To truly understand Sigma males, we must delve deep into their psyche, exploring the personality traits, motivations, and tendencies that shape their worldview and behaviors.

Independence as a Core Trait

One of the defining psychological aspects of Sigma males is their unwavering commitment to independence. Unlike Alphas, who often thrive in leadership roles, Sigma males have a strong aversion to hierarchies and a desire to forge their paths. This independence is rooted in a deep sense of self-reliance and a belief in the importance of charting one's course in life.

This desire for independence often leads Sigma males to resist societal norms and expectations. They are not motivated by the need for approval or validation from others but, instead, are driven by a profound sense of autonomy. This self-reliance is a central aspect of their psychological makeup and influences their decision-making and behavior.

Introversion and Self-Reflection

Another key psychological trait of Sigma males is introversion. They often find solace and strength in solitude, using their alone time for self-reflection and personal growth. Unlike extroverted Alphas who thrive in social settings, Sigma males are more inclined to recharge their energy in quiet and contemplative environments.

This introverted nature is not a sign of social anxiety or shyness but a deliberate choice to prioritize self-discovery and inner growth. Sigma males value the insights gained through introspection and see it as a source of strength and resilience.

Observational Skills and Perception

Sigma males tend to be keen observers of their environment. Their heightened sense of awareness allows them to read situations and people effectively, often making astute judgments and decisions. This observational skill is a result of their preference for silence and reflection, which enables them to take in information without the distractions of social interaction.

Their perceptive abilities are not limited to external observations but extend to understanding human behavior and motives. Sigma males often possess a knack for deciphering underlying dynamics in social and professional situations, giving them a unique advantage in navigating complex environments.

Silent Confidence and Self-Assuredness

Sigma males exude a distinct type of confidence, characterized by its quiet, understated nature. Unlike the overt confidence associated with Alphas, Sigma males radiate self-assuredness without the need for external validation. Their confidence is deeply rooted in their self-reliance and introspective nature.

This silent confidence is a psychological strength that enables Sigma males to stay true to their convictions and make decisions that align with their values, even in the face of opposition or skepticism. It is a source of inner strength that allows them to pursue their goals with determination and resilience.

Motivations and Drivers

Understanding the motivations and drivers of Sigma males is crucial to comprehending their psychological makeup. While each individual is unique, several common motivators underpin the actions and decisions of Sigma males:

1. **Freedom and Autonomy:** Sigma males are driven by a profound desire for freedom and autonomy. They seek to live life on their terms, free from the constraints of societal expectations and norms. This motivation fuels their independent spirit and nonconformist tendencies.

2. ***Authenticity:*** Authenticity is a core value for Sigma males. They are motivated to live in alignment with their true selves and resist any form of pretense or conformity. This authenticity extends to their relationships, pursuits, and life choices.

3. ***Personal Fulfillment:*** Sigma males are intrinsically motivated to pursue paths that bring them personal fulfillment and satisfaction. They prioritize their own happiness and well-being above external measures of success or approval.

4. ***Resilience:*** The self-reliance and introverted nature of Sigma males often stem from a desire to develop resilience. They see challenges and setbacks as opportunities for growth and personal development, motivating them to overcome adversity.

5. ***Influence and Impact:*** While not motivated by traditional forms of power and influence, Sigma males may be driven by a desire to make a meaningful impact on the world in their unique way. They seek to leave their mark through authenticity and self-expression.

Challenges and Tendencies

While Sigma males possess many strengths and positive psychological traits, they also face challenges and tendencies that are important to acknowledge:

1. **Difficulty in Forming Relationships:** Due to their introverted and independent nature, Sigma males may struggle to form and maintain relationships, especially with individuals who do not share their values or priorities.

2. **Resistance to Conformity:** Sigma males' strong aversion to conformity and societal norms can sometimes lead to conflicts and challenges, particularly in professional settings where conformity is expected.

3. **Isolation:** The preference for solitude and self-reflection can sometimes lead to isolation. Sigma males must strike a balance between their need for independence and their social connections to prevent loneliness.

4. **Risk of Misunderstanding:** Their quiet confidence and nonconformist tendencies may lead others to misunderstand or underestimate Sigma males. This can result in missed opportunities or unfulfilled potential.

5. **Introverted Challenges:** Introverted tendencies may make it challenging for Sigma males to assert themselves in social or professional

situations that require extroverted skills like networking or public speaking.

Conclusion: Embracing the Sigma Psyche

In conclusion, the psychological makeup of Sigma males is a complex and multifaceted terrain. Their independence, introversion, perceptive abilities, and silent confidence set them apart as a unique personality type. Understanding their motivations, strengths, and challenges is essential for both Sigma males themselves and those who interact with them.

Sigma males offer a valuable perspective on the importance of authenticity, self-reliance, and nonconformity in a world that often values extroversion and conformity. Embracing the Sigma psyche means recognizing and appreciating the richness of human diversity and the many paths to personal fulfillment and success.

The Sigma Male's Approach to Relationships: Navigating the Path of Independence and Connection

Relationships are the threads that weave the intricate fabric of human existence, and for Sigma males, these connections present both opportunities and challenges. Characterized by their independence, self-reliance, and nonconformist nature, Sigma males approach relationships in a unique and often enigmatic manner. In this exploration, we will delve into how Sigma males form and maintain relationships, the challenges they face, and the strategies they employ to foster healthy connections.

Defying Relationship Norms: The Sigma Way

For Sigma males, relationships are not a one-size-fits-all endeavor. They tend to defy traditional relationship norms and expectations, charting their paths to connection on their terms. This approach is rooted in their core values of independence and authenticity, making their relationships unconventional yet deeply meaningful.

Forming Relationships: Quality Over Quantity

Sigma males are selective when it comes to forming relationships. Unlike extroverted Alphas who may thrive in large social circles, Sigma males often prioritize quality over quantity. They are more likely to have a small, close-knit group of friends and acquaintances rather than a vast network of superficial connections.

When forming new relationships, Sigma males look for individuals who share their values, interests, and a mutual respect for independence. Authenticity and a sense of understanding are crucial factors in the initial stages of connection. These connections may develop slowly, as Sigma males tend to be cautious about letting others into their inner circle.

Maintaining Relationships: Balancing Independence and Connection

Maintaining relationships as a Sigma male can be a delicate balancing act. On one hand, they cherish their independence and solitude, needing time for self-reflection and personal growth. On the other hand, they value the connections they have and understand the importance of nurturing them.

To strike this balance, Sigma males often communicate openly with their friends, family, and romantic partners. They are honest about their need for alone time and self-reliance, ensuring that those close to them understand and respect these boundaries. This transparency helps prevent misunderstandings and conflicts.

Challenges in Building Connections

Despite their strengths, Sigma males encounter several challenges in building and maintaining relationships:

1. **Difficulty in Expressing Emotions:** Sigma males may struggle to express their emotions openly, which can make it challenging for their loved ones to understand their feelings and needs.

2. **Introverted Nature:** Their introverted tendencies can sometimes lead to isolation and difficulty in social situations that require extroverted skills, such as networking or group activities.

3. **Resistance to Conformity:** Sigma males' resistance to societal norms may create friction in relationships, especially if their partners or friends value conformity and tradition.

4. **Emotional Independence:** While emotional independence is a strength, it can also create emotional distance in relationships, making others feel neglected or unimportant.

5. **Communication Hurdles:** Sigma males may not be as verbally expressive as others, leading to misunderstandings or misinterpretations of their intentions.

Strategies for Healthy Connections

To overcome these challenges and foster healthy connections, Sigma males can employ several strategies:

1. ***Effective Communication:*** Sigma males should work on improving their communication skills, expressing their feelings and needs clearly and directly. Regular check-ins with loved ones can help bridge emotional gaps.

2. ***Setting Boundaries:*** Establishing clear boundaries and expectations in relationships is crucial. Sigma males should communicate their need for alone time while ensuring that their loved ones feel valued and appreciated.

3. ***Shared Interests:*** Finding and nurturing relationships with individuals who share common interests can provide a foundation for connection. Shared activities can serve as bridges for emotional connection.

4. ***Empathy and Understanding:*** Sigma males should actively practice empathy and understanding, acknowledging that not everyone shares their worldview. This can help them navigate conflicts and differences with more grace.

5. ***Embracing Vulnerability:*** While Sigma males value self-reliance, they can benefit from embracing vulnerability when appropriate. Sharing their thoughts and emotions can create deeper connections with others.

6. **Compromise:** Recognizing that compromise is a part of any relationship can help Sigma males navigate situations where their independence conflicts with the needs of their loved ones.

7. **Seeking Support:** When facing relationship challenges, seeking support from trusted friends, therapists, or relationship counselors can provide valuable insights and guidance.

Conclusion: The Enigmatic Harmony of Sigma Relationships

The Sigma male's approach to relationships is a dance of independence and connection, a balance of solitude and togetherness. While they may defy traditional norms, Sigma males offer a unique perspective on the importance of authenticity and meaningful connections.

In the intricate web of human relationships, Sigma males remind us that there is no one-size-fits-all approach. Their nonconformist spirit challenges us to question societal expectations and embrace the diversity of human connections. By navigating the path of independence and connection with mindfulness and empathy, Sigma males can cultivate relationships that are as authentic as they are enigmatic.

Success and Achievement Strategies for Sigma Males: Thriving on Their Own Terms

Success is a multifaceted concept, and Sigma males approach it in their unique, often unconventional way. Their independence, self-reliance, and nonconformist nature drive them to chart their paths to success on their terms. In this exploration, we will investigate the distinct strategies Sigma males employ to achieve their goals and offer advice on setting and attaining both personal and professional success.

1. Defining Success on Their Terms

Sigma males tend to have a deeply personal and individualistic definition of success. Rather than adhering to societal expectations or chasing external markers of achievement, they prioritize their own values and fulfillment. Their first step toward success is to define what it means to them personally.

Advice: Take the time to reflect on your core values, passions, and aspirations. What does success look like for you? By setting your own standards, you can create a roadmap that aligns with your authentic self.

2. Leveraging Independence and Self-Reliance

One of the strengths of Sigma males lies in their self-reliance and independence. They are not afraid to pursue their goals alone, and this quality allows them to take calculated risks and make independent decisions.

Advice: Embrace your independence and self-reliance as assets. Use them to your advantage by taking calculated risks and making decisions that align with your long-term vision. Don't be afraid to chart your course.

3. Goal Setting and Planning

Sigma males approach goal setting with a methodical and strategic mindset. They often set ambitious, well-defined goals and develop detailed plans to achieve them. Their goal-setting process is driven by their inner sense of purpose.

Advice: When setting goals, be specific, measurable, and time-bound (SMART). Create a detailed plan outlining the steps required to reach your objectives. Regularly review and adjust your plans as needed.

4. Embracing Failure as a Learning Opportunity

Sigma males understand that failure is an inevitable part of the journey to success. They don't fear setbacks; instead, they view them as valuable learning experiences. This mindset allows them to adapt and grow.

Advice. Embrace failure as a teacher, not a deterrent. Analyze your setbacks to uncover lessons and insights.

Use these experiences to refine your strategies and move closer to your goals.

5. Networking with Purpose

While Sigma males may not be natural networkers, they recognize the value of meaningful connections. They prioritize building relationships with individuals who share their values and can contribute to their goals.

Advice: Focus on quality, not quantity, when building your network. Seek out individuals who align with your objectives and can provide support, guidance, or collaboration opportunities.

6. Emphasizing Self-Care and Balance

Maintaining a healthy work-life balance is crucial for Sigma males. They understand that success is not solely defined by professional achievements and prioritize self-care and well-being.

Advice: Make self-care a non-negotiable part of your routine. Dedicate time to recharge, whether through hobbies, exercise, meditation, or quality time with loved ones. A well-balanced life enhances overall success.

7. Patience and Persistence

Sigma males exhibit a remarkable degree of patience and persistence on their journey to success. They understand that meaningful achievements often take time and effort.

Advice: Stay committed to your goals, even when progress feels slow. Trust the process and remain persistent in your pursuit. Small, consistent efforts can lead to significant outcomes over time.

8. Staying True to Authenticity

Sigma males never compromise their authenticity for the sake of success. They recognize that genuine success is only meaningful when achieved while staying true to one's values and identity.

Advice: Stay true to yourself throughout your journey. Don't conform to external expectations or societal norms. Authentic success is the most fulfilling kind.

9. Celebrating Achievements

Sigma males often downplay their successes, but celebrating achievements is essential for motivation and a sense of accomplishment. Recognize and reward yourself for your hard work and progress.

Advice: Acknowledge your achievements, no matter how small. Celebrate milestones along the way to keep yourself motivated and remind yourself of your progress.

10. Continuous Learning and Adaptation

Sigma males are lifelong learners who understand that growth and success require adaptability. They are open to acquiring new skills, knowledge, and perspectives.

Advice: Foster a growth mindset by embracing opportunities for learning and development. Be open to change and adaptation as you pursue your goals. Continual growth is a hallmark of success.

In conclusion, Sigma males have a unique and effective approach to success and achievement. By defining success on their terms, leveraging their independence, setting well-planned goals, and embracing failure as a learning opportunity, they navigate the path to success with determination and authenticity. By incorporating these strategies into your own journey, you can thrive and achieve your personal and professional goals while staying true to your authentic self. Success, as a Sigma male knows, is not solely about the destination but also about the journey itself.

The Art of Independence: Nurturing the Sigma Male's Self-Reliance

Independence and self-reliance are the cornerstones of the Sigma male's identity. Unlike the conventional path of conforming to societal norms or seeking external validation, Sigma males embrace the art of independence, allowing them to forge their paths with authenticity and determination. In this exploration, we will delve into the Sigma male's inclination towards independence, offering guidance on developing and maintaining self-sufficiency.

Understanding the Sigma Male's Independence

Sigma males are known for their unwavering commitment to independence. It is a core aspect of their identity and shapes many aspects of their lives. To understand this trait better, let's explore its foundations and manifestations:

1. ***Autonomy:*** Sigma males value autonomy and self-direction. They prefer to make decisions independently and rely on their judgment rather than seeking external guidance.

2. ***Self-Reliance:*** Self-reliance is a fundamental principle for Sigma males. They take pride in their ability to solve problems, overcome challenges, and meet their needs without relying heavily on others.

3. **Nonconformity:** Independence often leads Sigma males to resist conformity and societal norms. They have a natural inclination to question established rules and authority.

4. **Inner Drive:** Sigma males are intrinsically motivated and driven by personal fulfillment rather than external rewards or recognition. They pursue their goals with passion and determination.

5. **Embracing Solitude:** While Sigma males can form deep and meaningful relationships, they also cherish solitude. They use alone time for self-reflection, personal growth, and rejuvenation.

Guidance on Developing Self-Sufficiency

Self-sufficiency is a skill that Sigma males continuously refine and hone. It enables them to navigate life's challenges with confidence and adaptability. Here are some strategies to develop and maintain self-sufficiency:

1. **Cultivate Problem-Solving Skills:** Enhance your problem-solving abilities by seeking out challenges and actively working through solutions. The more you practice, the more adept you become at handling complex situations.

2. **Learn New Skills:** Continual learning is a hallmark of self-sufficiency. Acquire new skills and knowledge that align with your interests and goals. This expands your capabilities and independence.

3. **Set Clear Goals:** Establish well-defined goals that reflect your values and aspirations. A clear sense of purpose provides direction and motivation for your independent pursuits.

4. **Seek Feedback and Mentorship:** While Sigma males value self-reliance, they can benefit from feedback and mentorship. Trusted advisors or mentors can offer valuable insights and guidance on your journey.

5. **Embrace Adversity:** Rather than avoiding challenges, confront them head-on. Adversity is a powerful teacher that can enhance your problem-solving skills and resilience.

6. **Build Financial Independence:** Financial stability is a key aspect of self-sufficiency. Develop good financial habits, save, invest wisely, and live within your means to secure your financial future.

7. **Prioritize Self-Care:** Self-sufficiency includes taking care of your physical and mental well-being. Prioritize self-care practices like exercise,

meditation, and a healthy lifestyle to maintain your resilience.

Maintaining Independence in Relationships

While independence is a vital aspect of the Sigma male's identity, it doesn't mean they cannot form meaningful relationships. Balancing independence with connection is essential for their overall well-being. Here's how:

1. **Set Boundaries:** Clearly communicate your need for independence and solitude with loved ones. Establishing boundaries ensures that you have the space and time you require.

2. **Choose Compatible Partners:** Seek out partners who appreciate and respect your independence. A compatible partner will support your individuality and encourage your growth.

3. **Nurture Empathy and Communication:** Work on your empathetic and communication skills to bridge any emotional gaps in relationships. Open and honest communication is key to maintaining connections.

4. **Quality Over Quantity:** Prioritize quality relationships over a large social circle. Invest in deep and meaningful connections with individuals who share your values and support your independence.

5. ***Maintain Self-Identity:*** Ensure that your relationships do not overshadow your sense of self. Continue to pursue your interests and passions independently.

Conclusion: The Empowering Path of Independence

The art of independence for Sigma males is an empowering journey of self-discovery and personal growth. By embracing autonomy, self-reliance, and nonconformity, they pave the way for a life that reflects their authentic selves. Developing self-sufficiency and maintaining independence in relationships are vital aspects of this journey. It is a path that allows Sigma males to thrive on their terms, charting their course through the complexities of life with confidence and authenticity.

Mastering the Art of Social Skills and Effective Communication: A Guide to Thriving in a Diverse World

In the intricate web of human interactions, social skills and effective communication serve as the threads that connect us all. These skills are not only essential for building meaningful relationships but also for navigating the diverse tapestry of personalities that populate our world. In this comprehensive exploration, we will delve into strategies for improving social skills and communication while providing practical tips for interacting with individuals of various personality archetypes, including Alphas, Betas, and others.

The Significance of Social Skills and Communication

Before delving into strategies and tips, it's crucial to understand the profound importance of social skills and effective communication in our lives:

1. **Building Relationships:** Social skills are the foundation of building and maintaining meaningful relationships, whether personal or professional. They foster trust, empathy, and connection with others.

2. **Navigating Diversity:** In today's diverse world, effective communication is essential for

connecting with individuals from different backgrounds, cultures, and personality types. It helps bridge gaps and foster understanding.

3. **Conflict Resolution:** Good communication skills are vital for resolving conflicts, whether they arise in personal relationships, the workplace, or other settings. Effective communication can prevent misunderstandings and facilitate resolution.

4. **Career Advancement:** In the professional realm, strong communication skills are often the difference between success and stagnation. They enable effective collaboration, leadership, and negotiation.

5. **Personal Growth:** Improving social skills and communication fosters personal growth by enhancing self-awareness, emotional intelligence, and adaptability.

Now, let's explore strategies to enhance social skills and communication and practical tips for interacting with individuals representing different personality archetypes.

Strategies for Improving Social Skills and Communication

1. **Active Listening:** Active listening is the foundation of effective communication. Practice

listening without interruption, showing empathy, and asking clarifying questions to understand the speaker's perspective fully.

2. **Develop Empathy:** Cultivate empathy by putting yourself in others' shoes. Try to understand their feelings and viewpoints, even if they differ from your own. Empathy enhances understanding and connection.

3. **Body Language Awareness:** Pay attention to nonverbal cues such as facial expressions, posture, and gestures. Maintain open and approachable body language to convey your interest and receptivity.

4. **Verbal Communication:** Practice clear and concise verbal communication. Avoid jargon or overly complex language, especially when communicating with a diverse audience. Tailor your message to your audience's level of understanding.

5. **Mindful Speech:** Think before you speak. Mindful speech involves choosing words carefully to convey your message accurately and respectfully. Avoid hurtful or offensive language.

6. **Conflict Resolution Skills:** Learn effective conflict resolution techniques, such as active listening, finding common ground, and seeking

compromise. Address conflicts calmly and constructively.

7. ***Feedback and Self-Reflection:*** Seek feedback from others to identify areas for improvement in your communication. Engage in self-reflection to assess your strengths and weaknesses.

8. ***Adapt to Different Styles:*** Recognize that people have different communication styles. Adapt your approach to align with the preferences and needs of the person you are communicating with.

9. ***Practice Empathetic Communication:*** When someone shares their thoughts or concerns, respond empathetically by acknowledging their feelings and expressing understanding. Avoid rushing to provide solutions unless asked.

Practical Tips for Interacting with Alphas

Alpha personalities are often characterized by dominance, assertiveness, and confidence. Interacting with Alphas can be dynamic and challenging. Here are some tips:

1. ***Respect Their Confidence:*** Alphas value confidence and assertiveness. Show respect for their self-assured nature, even if it contrasts with your own style.

2. ***Be Direct:*** Alphas appreciate direct communication. Avoid ambiguity and speak your mind clearly when interacting with them.

3. ***Highlight Mutual Goals:*** Find common goals or objectives to align with Alphas. They appreciate collaboration that leads to tangible outcomes.

4. ***Don't Back Down:*** While respecting their dominance, don't be afraid to stand your ground when necessary. Alphas respect individuals who can hold their own.

5. ***Acknowledge Their Achievements:*** Recognize and appreciate their accomplishments and contributions. Alphas thrive on acknowledgment and recognition.

Practical Tips for Interacting with Betas

Beta personalities tend to be accommodating, cooperative, and less assertive. Interacting with Betas requires sensitivity and understanding. Here are some tips:

1. ***Show Patience:*** Betas may take longer to express themselves or make decisions. Be patient and allow them the time they need.

2. ***Encourage Their Input:*** Actively seek their opinions and ideas in group settings. Betas often have valuable insights to offer.

3. ***Offer Support:*** Betas appreciate support and encouragement. Be a source of reassurance and positivity in their endeavors.

4. ***Avoid Overwhelming Them:*** Be mindful not to overwhelm Betas with assertiveness or dominance. Create a comfortable and inclusive environment.

5. ***Appreciate Their Teamwork:*** Recognize and praise their teamwork and cooperative nature. They thrive in environments that value collaboration.

Practical Tips for Interacting with Others

Beyond Alphas and Betas, the world is full of diverse personalities. Here are some general tips for interacting effectively with others:

1. ***Respect Differences:*** Embrace the diversity of personalities and backgrounds. Respect others' viewpoints and beliefs, even if they differ from your own.

2. ***Practice Cultural Sensitivity:*** In multicultural settings, be mindful of cultural differences in communication styles and customs. Show respect for diverse traditions and norms.

3. ***Tailor Your Communication:*** Adapt your communication style to suit the preferences and

needs of the individual or group you are interacting with. Flexibility is key.

4. **Ask Open-Ended Questions:** Encourage meaningful conversations by asking open-ended questions that invite discussion and reflection.

5. **Show Appreciation:** Express gratitude and appreciation for others' contributions and perspectives. A culture of appreciation fosters positive relationships.

6. **Handle Disagreements Gracefully:** Disagreements are inevitable. Approach them with grace and a willingness to find common ground or compromise.

Conclusion: A Compass for Effective Communication

Social skills and effective communication are the compass that guides us through the complex terrain of human interactions. By mastering these skills, we not only build meaningful relationships but also foster understanding and collaboration in our diverse world. Whether interacting with Alphas, Betas, or individuals of various personality archetypes, the strategies and practical tips outlined here serve as valuable tools for thriving in a richly diverse and interconnected society. Communication is not merely a means of conveying information; it is the bridge that connects us all.

Embracing Silence and Solitude: The Sigma Male's Path to Inner Strength

In a world that often celebrates extroversion, constant connectivity, and social engagement, the Sigma male stands as a beacon of independence and self-reliance. At the heart of the Sigma male's unique identity is a profound comfort with silence and solitude. While society may perceive solitude as isolation, the Sigma male recognizes it as a powerful source of inner strength and growth. In this comprehensive exploration, we will highlight the Sigma male's affinity for solitude, delve into the benefits of alone time and self-reflection, and unveil the wisdom that can be gained from embracing silence and solitude.

Understanding the Sigma Male's Comfort with Solitude

The Sigma male's comfort with solitude is rooted in their core characteristics and values. To grasp this affinity better, let's examine the key elements that define their relationship with solitude:

1. **Independence:** Sigma males prioritize independence and self-reliance. They are comfortable making decisions and pursuing their goals on their terms, often without seeking external validation or approval.

2. ***Introversion:*** Many Sigma males lean towards introversion. While not all are introverts, a significant number find solace in quiet and contemplative environments, where they can recharge and reflect.

3. ***Self-Reflection:*** Sigma males recognize the value of self-reflection. They use their alone time to explore their thoughts, feelings, and experiences, seeking to understand themselves better and refine their sense of identity.

4. ***Authenticity:*** Authenticity is a central value for Sigma males. They prioritize living in alignment with their true selves and resist pretense or conformity to fit societal expectations.

5. ***Observational Skills:*** Sigma males often possess keen observational skills. Their heightened awareness allows them to observe and understand their environment and the people around them more effectively.

The Benefits of Alone Time and Self-Reflection

Solitude is not mere isolation for Sigma males; it is a deliberate choice that brings forth a wealth of benefits for personal growth and well-being:

1. ***Clarity of Thought:*** Alone time provides the mental space necessary for clear and focused thinking. Sigma males use this clarity to assess

their goals, make decisions, and develop strategies for success.

2. ***Self-Discovery:*** Solitude allows for introspection and self-discovery. Sigma males use this time to explore their values, interests, strengths, weaknesses, and personal aspirations.

3. ***Emotional Regulation:*** Self-reflection fosters emotional intelligence. Sigma males gain a better understanding of their emotions and learn to manage them effectively, which is invaluable in both personal and professional life.

4. ***Enhanced Problem-Solving:*** Solitude fosters critical thinking and problem-solving skills. Sigma males can approach challenges with a fresh perspective, untainted by external influences.

5. ***Creativity and Innovation:*** Many groundbreaking ideas and innovations have emerged during moments of solitude. Sigma males harness their creative potential when they allow their minds to wander freely.

6. ***Stress Reduction:*** Solitude serves as a refuge from the demands and stressors of daily life. It offers a respite for relaxation and stress reduction, promoting mental and emotional well-being.

Navigating the Sigma Male's Relationship with Solitude

While solitude offers numerous advantages, it's essential for Sigma males to navigate this relationship skillfully to reap its benefits fully. Here are some strategies for embracing and harnessing solitude effectively:

1. **Establish a Routine:** Create a daily or weekly routine that includes dedicated alone time for self-reflection and relaxation. Consistency helps make solitude a regular and essential part of your life.

2. **Find a Comfortable Space:** Identify a space where you feel most comfortable and at ease during alone time. It could be a quiet room, a natural setting, or a cozy corner in your home.

3. **Limit Distractions:** Minimize external distractions during your alone time. Turn off electronic devices, put away work-related materials, and create a peaceful environment that promotes inner reflection.

4. **Set Intentions:** Approach your alone time with intention. Define what you want to achieve during this time, whether it's self-reflection, problem-solving, or creative exploration.

5. **Practice Mindfulness:** Embrace mindfulness techniques such as meditation or deep breathing exercises. These practices enhance self-awareness and can deepen your connection with solitude.

6. **Record Your Thoughts:** Keep a journal or use digital tools to record your thoughts, insights, and reflections during your alone time. This helps you track your personal growth and development.

7. **Engage in Creative Pursuits:** Use solitude as an opportunity to engage in creative activities that you enjoy, whether it's writing, painting, playing music, or any other form of self-expression.

8. **Seek Guidance:** Consider seeking guidance from mentors, counselors, or therapists to enhance your self-reflection and personal development journey.

The Wisdom Gained from Embracing Silence and Solitude

Embracing solitude is not a retreat from the world; rather, it is a journey inward, a quest for self-discovery, and a source of profound wisdom. Here are some insights that can be gained from the Sigma male's affinity for silence and solitude.

1. ***Self-Acceptance:*** Solitude fosters self-acceptance. Sigma males learn to embrace their true selves, appreciating their strengths and acknowledging their areas for growth.

2. ***Resilience:*** Solitude enhances emotional resilience. Sigma males gain the strength to face challenges, setbacks, and adversity with composure and determination.

3. ***Inner Peace:*** Solitude often leads to a sense of inner peace and contentment. Sigma males find solace in their own company, free from the noise and distractions of the external world.

4. ***Deeper Relationships:*** Paradoxically, solitude can lead to more meaningful connections with others. Sigma males bring their authentic selves into relationships, fostering deeper and more genuine connections.

5. ***Wisdom and Insight:*** Through self-reflection, Sigma males gain profound wisdom and insight into the human experience, which can guide them in making informed decisions and navigating life's complexities.

Conclusion: The Journey Inward

In a world that often values constant connectivity and social engagement, the Sigma male's comfort with solitude stands as a testament to the power of inner reflection and self-discovery. Solitude is not a path of isolation; it is a journey inward, a quest for authenticity and wisdom, and a source of inner strength. By embracing silence and solitude, Sigma males exemplify the profound benefits that can be gained from exploring the depths of one's own soul. It is a journey that teaches us that sometimes, the most meaningful connection is the one we forge with ourselves.

Navigating the Sigma Male Journey: Challenges and Misconceptions Unveiled

The Sigma male, with his distinctive blend of independence, self-reliance, and nonconformity, exists as a multifaceted enigma in a world often defined by social hierarchies and archetypes. While Sigma males possess unique strengths and perspectives, they also encounter a range of challenges and misconceptions that shape their experiences. In this comprehensive exploration, we will shine a light on the common misconceptions surrounding Sigma males and delve into the challenges they face, offering valuable insights on overcoming these obstacles.

Common Misconceptions About Sigma Males

To understand the Sigma male's journey better, it's crucial to address some prevalent misconceptions:

1. Misconception: Sigma Males are Simply Introverts

- Reality: While many Sigma males lean toward introversion, not all are introverts. Their core traits encompass independence, self-reliance, and nonconformity, making them more complex than a single personality label.

2. Misconception: Sigma Males Are Always Lone Wolves

- Reality: Sigma males value meaningful connections but on their terms. They form relationships selectively, prioritizing quality over quantity.

3. Misconception: Sigma Males Are Anti-Social

- Reality: Sigma males are not anti-social; they simply have a different approach to socializing. They may prefer smaller gatherings or one-on-one interactions over large social events.

4. Misconception: Sigma Males Lack Emotion or Empathy

- Reality: Sigma males experience emotions like anyone else, but they may not always express them openly. They often have a deep sense of empathy and understanding, especially in close relationships.

5. Misconception: Sigma Males Are Rebels Without a Cause

- Reality: Sigma males may resist conformity and challenge societal norms, but their actions are often driven by a strong sense of authenticity, not mere rebellion.

6. Misconception: Sigma Males Don't Seek Success or Ambition

- Reality: Sigma males are highly ambitious and goal-oriented. They define success on their terms and are often self-motivated to achieve their objectives.

Challenges Faced by Sigma Males

The Sigma male journey is marked by unique challenges that arise from their nonconformist nature and independent spirit:

1. Difficulty in Forming Connections:

- Challenge: Sigma males may struggle to initiate and maintain connections due to their selective nature and resistance to traditional social norms.

- Insight: Actively seek out individuals who share your values and interests. Focus on developing quality relationships with those who align with your authentic self.

2. Misperceptions and Stereotyping:

- Challenge: Society's preconceived notions and stereotypes about Sigma males can lead to misunderstanding and judgment.

- Insight: Educate those around you about your values and perspectives. Foster open communication to dispel misconceptions.

3. Isolation and Loneliness:

- Challenge: Embracing solitude can sometimes lead to feelings of isolation and loneliness, especially if Sigma males lack a support system that understands their needs.

- Insight: Nurture a small, close-knit group of friends and acquaintances who respect your independence. Seek support from like-minded individuals who value authenticity.

4. Conflict with Conformity:

- Challenge: Sigma males often face societal pressure to conform to traditional expectations, which can create internal conflict.

- Insight: Stay true to your authentic self while recognizing when flexibility is necessary. Focus on the aspects of conformity that align with your values and goals.

5. Misunderstood Emotions:

- Challenge: Sigma males may struggle to express their emotions openly, leading to misunderstandings in relationships.

- Insight: Practice open communication and express your feelings in ways that feel comfortable to you. Encourage loved ones to ask questions and seek clarification.

6. Limited Social Opportunities:

- Challenge: Traditional social gatherings and events may not align with the preferences of Sigma males, limiting their opportunities for connection.

- Insight: Seek out alternative social opportunities that cater to your interests and preferences. Attend smaller gatherings or engage in activities that resonate with you.

Overcoming Challenges and Thriving as a Sigma Male

Facing challenges head-on is integral to the Sigma male journey. Here are valuable insights and strategies to overcome obstacles and thrive:

1. Self-Acceptance:

- Embrace your Sigma male identity with pride. Recognize that your uniqueness is a strength, not a weakness.

2. Effective Communication:

- Practice clear and open communication with those around you. Explain your needs, boundaries, and values to foster understanding.

3. Seek Like-Minded Communities:

- Connect with individuals who share your values and perspectives. Online communities, forums, and social groups can offer valuable support.

4. Adaptability:

- Develop the ability to adapt when necessary. Recognize that there may be situations where conformity or compromise is in your best interest.

5. Emotional Expression:

- Work on expressing your emotions in ways that feel authentic to you. Seek guidance from professionals or trusted individuals if needed.

6. Pursue Personal Growth:

- Continue to pursue personal growth and self-improvement. Set and achieve goals that align with your values and ambitions.

7. Embrace Solitude Mindfully:

- Embrace solitude as a source of strength and self-discovery. Utilize alone time for self-reflection and rejuvenation.

8. Educate Others:

- Take the initiative to educate others about your personality type and values. Encourage open dialogue and dispel misconceptions.

9. Build Resilience:

- Cultivate emotional resilience to navigate challenges effectively. Develop coping strategies that align with your personality.

10. Forge Meaningful Connections: - Focus on building deep, meaningful connections with individuals who appreciate your authenticity and independence.

Conclusion: The Unveiled Sigma Male Journey

The Sigma male journey is one of resilience, authenticity, and self-discovery. While challenges and misconceptions may shape their path, Sigma males have the strength and determination to overcome obstacles and thrive on their terms. By embracing their unique identity and forging genuine connections, Sigma males can navigate a world of conformity with grace and authenticity, leaving a lasting impact defined by their unwavering independence and self-reliance.

Sigma Male Role Models: Defying Conventions and Shaping the World

In a world often captivated by the charisma of Alpha males and the steady reliability of Beta males, Sigma males stand as unique and enigmatic figures. With their penchant for independence, self-reliance, and nonconformity, Sigma males forge their paths and leave their mark on the world in distinctive ways. In this exploration, we will profile real-life Sigma male role models from various fields, showcasing their remarkable achievements and the characteristics that define them as exceptional individuals.

1. Nikola Tesla: The Innovator of the Electrical Age

Achievements:

- Nikola Tesla, a Serbian-American inventor, engineer, and futurist, is best known for his pioneering work in electrical engineering and his contributions to the development of alternating current (AC) electrical systems.

- He held over 300 patents, including those for the Tesla coil and the radio remote control, and made groundbreaking advancements in wireless communication and transmission of electricity.

Sigma Male Characteristics:

- Independence: Tesla's visionary ideas often led him to work independently, even when it meant going against the prevailing scientific and engineering norms of his time.

- Introversion: He was known for his solitary lifestyle and relentless focus on his work, often preferring solitude for creativity and innovation.

- Nonconformity: Tesla challenged established conventions, particularly in his advocacy for AC power over direct current (DC), which led to the "War of Currents" with Thomas Edison.

2. Albert Einstein: The Genius Behind the Theory of Relativity

Achievements:

- Albert Einstein, a German-born physicist, revolutionized our understanding of the universe with his theory of relativity, which fundamentally altered the fields of physics and cosmology.

- He was awarded the Nobel Prize in Physics in 1921 for his explanation of the photoelectric effect and made lasting contributions to the development of quantum mechanics.

Sigma Male Characteristics:

- Independence: Einstein often pursued his research independently, famously working as a patent examiner during his "miracle year" of scientific breakthroughs.

- Introversion: He was known for his introverted personality, and his deep thinking and thought experiments often took place in solitude.

- Nonconformity: Einstein's theories challenged classical physics and introduced radical new concepts, making him a nonconformist in the scientific community.

3. Warren Buffett: The Oracle of Omaha

Achievements:

- Warren Buffett is one of the most successful investors in history, known for his long-term, value-oriented approach to investing. He is the chairman and CEO of Berkshire Hathaway.

- Buffett's wealth and influence have earned him the nickname "The Oracle of Omaha," and he is celebrated for his philanthropy and commitment to giving away the majority of his fortune.

Sigma Male Characteristics:

- Independence: Buffett has maintained an independent investment philosophy, often going against market trends and maintaining a long-term perspective.

- Introversion: Despite his immense success, Buffett remains introverted, preferring a simple and low-key lifestyle.

- Nonconformity: His investment strategy of "value investing" runs counter to the prevailing wisdom of short-term speculation and market timing.

4. Elon Musk: The Visionary Entrepreneur Pushing Boundaries

Achievements:

- Elon Musk, a South African-born entrepreneur, is known for his transformative ventures in the technology and space exploration industries.

- He co-founded PayPal, launched electric car manufacturer Tesla, founded SpaceX, and is behind the development of the Hyperloop and the Neuralink project.

Sigma Male Characteristics:

- Independence: Musk has a reputation for being a fiercely independent thinker and entrepreneur, willing to take significant risks to achieve his ambitious goals.

- Introversion: While his public persona may suggest extroversion, Musk's introspective and contemplative nature is evident in his relentless pursuit of innovative solutions.

- Nonconformity: Musk's companies are known for challenging established industries and norms, from electric vehicles to space exploration.

5. Bruce Lee: The Martial Arts Icon and Philosopher

Achievements:

- Bruce Lee was a martial artist, actor, and philosopher who revolutionized martial arts with his Jeet Kune Do philosophy and contributed significantly to the popularization of martial arts in the West.

- He starred in iconic films like "Enter the Dragon" and "Way of the Dragon" and became a cultural icon.

Sigma Male Characteristics:

- Independence: Lee was known for developing his martial arts philosophy, Jeet Kune Do, which emphasized simplicity, directness, and personal expression.

- Introversion: He engaged in deep self-reflection and philosophy, authoring books like "Tao of Jeet Kune Do" and "The Warrior Within."

- Nonconformity: Lee challenged traditional martial arts styles, advocating adaptability and continuous self-improvement.

6. J.K. Rowling: The Author of the Wizarding World

Achievements:

- J.K. Rowling, a British author, is best known for creating the beloved Harry Potter series, which has captivated readers of all ages worldwide.

- Her books have sold over 500 million copies and inspired films, merchandise, and theme park attractions.

Sigma Male Characteristics:

- Independence: Rowling's journey as a writer included periods of solitude and self-reliance, during which she crafted the intricate world of Harry Potter.

- Introversion: She has described herself as an introvert and has spoken about the importance of quiet and solitude for creativity.

- Nonconformity: Rowling's books challenged the conventions of children's literature and storytelling, introducing complex characters and moral themes.

7. Clint Eastwood: The Actor and Filmmaker Extraordinaire

Achievements:

- Clint Eastwood is an iconic American actor, director, and producer known for his roles in classic films like "Dirty Harry," "Unforgiven," and "Million Dollar Baby."

- He has received numerous awards for his work, including Academy Awards for Best Director.

Sigma Male Characteristics:

- Independence: Eastwood has often chosen roles and projects independently, demonstrating a strong sense of artistic control and vision.

- Introversion: He is known for his reserved and introspective demeanor, both on and off-screen.

- Nonconformity: Eastwood's films often explore unconventional and morally complex themes, challenging traditional Hollywood narratives.

8. Richard Feynman: The Playful Physicist and Nobel Laureate

Achievements:

- Richard Feynman was an American theoretical physicist known for his contributions to quantum mechanics and quantum electrodynamics.

- He received the Nobel Prize in Physics in 1965 for his work in the field of quantum electrodynamics and became renowned for his engaging lectures and books.

Sigma Male Characteristics:

- Independence: Feynman's approach to physics and scientific problem-solving was characterized by his independent thinking and unique perspective.

- Introversion: Despite his charisma as a lecturer, Feynman was known for his introverted and contemplative nature.

- Nonconformity: His unorthodox teaching methods and ability to communicate complex ideas in simple terms made him a nonconformist in the world of academia.

9. Ayn Rand: The Philosopher and Novelist

Achievements:

- Ayn Rand, a Russian-American philosopher and novelist, is best known for her philosophical works, "The Fountainhead" and "Atlas Shrugged."

- Her philosophy of Objectivism has influenced political and economic discourse and has a devoted following.

Sigma Male Characteristics:

- Independence: Rand's philosophical and literary work reflects her unwavering commitment to individualism and self-reliance.

- Introversion: She was known for her intellectual and introspective nature, which is evident in her complex and thought-provoking novels.

- Nonconformity: Rand's philosophy challenged prevailing collectivist ideologies, advocating for the primacy of individual rights and values.

10. Christopher Nolan: The Visionary Filmmaker

Achievements:

- Christopher Nolan is a British-American filmmaker known for his groundbreaking and critically acclaimed films, including "Inception," "The Dark Knight Trilogy," and "Interstellar."

- His films have pushed the boundaries of storytelling and visual effects, earning numerous awards and accolades.

Sigma Male Characteristics:

- Independence: Nolan has maintained creative independence, often writing, directing, and producing his films, resulting in a distinctive cinematic style.

- Introversion: He is known for his introspective and enigmatic approach to storytelling, inviting audiences to engage with complex narratives.

- Nonconformity: Nolan's films often explore unconventional themes, timelines, and structures, challenging the conventions of mainstream cinema.

Conclusion: The Unconventional Trailblazers

Sigma male role models, drawn from diverse fields and backgrounds, exemplify the power of independence, nonconformity, and self-reliance. They have challenged conventions, pushed boundaries, and left an indelible mark on the world through their remarkable achievements. These individuals showcase that the Sigma male journey is one of embracing one's uniqueness and carving a path guided by authenticity, determination, and visionary thinking. They serve as inspirations not only for Sigma males but for anyone who dares to challenge the status quo and forge their own extraordinary legacy.

Embarking on the Journey of Self-Discovery and Personal Growth: Unleash Your Potential

The journey of self-discovery and personal growth is a profound expedition into the depths of your own being—a quest to understand your true self, unleash your potential, and live a more fulfilling life. In a world filled with external distractions and societal expectations, this exploration is not just valuable but essential. In this comprehensive guide, we will encourage you to embark on this transformative journey and provide you with the tools, exercises, and insights needed to embark on your own path of self-discovery and personal growth.

The Significance of Self-Discovery and Personal Growth

Before we delve into the practical aspects of self-discovery and personal growth, let's first understand why this journey is so vital.

1. **Authenticity:** Self-discovery is about uncovering your authentic self—your values, beliefs, passions, and aspirations. It empowers you to live a life that aligns with who you truly are.

2. **Fulfillment:** Personal growth leads to a greater sense of fulfillment and happiness. When you continuously develop and learn, you're more

likely to find purpose and satisfaction in your life.

3. **Resilience:** Understanding yourself better equips you to navigate life's challenges with greater resilience and adaptability. You become better at managing stress and overcoming setbacks.

4. **Healthy Relationships:** Self-discovery improves your relationships. When you know yourself well, you can communicate effectively, set healthy boundaries, and form deeper connections with others.

5. **Achievement:** Personal growth enhances your ability to set and achieve goals. It allows you to tap into your potential and reach new heights in various areas of your life.

Embracing the Journey of Self-Discovery

Embarking on the journey of self-discovery requires commitment, curiosity, and an open heart and mind. Here's how you can get started:

1. Cultivate Self-Awareness:

- Self-awareness is the cornerstone of self-discovery. Start by asking yourself fundamental questions: What are your core values? What are your strengths and weaknesses? What brings you joy and fulfillment?

- Journaling: Maintain a journal to record your thoughts, feelings, and reflections. Regular journaling can help you gain clarity about your inner world.

2. Embrace Mindfulness:

- Mindfulness involves being fully present in the moment without judgment. It allows you to observe your thoughts and feelings without attachment.

- Meditation: Practice mindfulness meditation to develop your awareness and cultivate a deeper connection with your inner self.

3. Seek Feedback:

- Feedback from trusted friends, family members, or mentors can provide valuable insights into your strengths and areas for improvement. Be open to constructive criticism.

4. Explore Your Passions:

- Identify your passions and interests. What activities make you lose track of time? What brings you joy? Dedicate time to pursue these passions.

5. Face Your Fears:

- Self-discovery often involves confronting your fears and limiting beliefs. Identify the fears that hold you back and work on overcoming them.

6. Reflect on Your Life Story:

- Your life experiences, both positive and negative, shape your identity. Reflect on your past experiences and how they have influenced your values and beliefs.

Tools and Exercises for Personal Growth

Once you've begun your journey of self-discovery, it's time to embark on the path of personal growth. Here are practical tools and exercises to guide you on this transformative journey:

1. Set Clear Goals:

- Goal setting is a powerful tool for personal growth. Define specific, measurable, achievable, relevant, and time-bound (SMART) goals that align with your values and aspirations.

2. Develop a Growth Mindset:

- Embrace a growth mindset, which is the belief that your abilities and intelligence can be developed through effort and learning.

- Challenge negative self-talk and replace it with affirmations that promote growth and resilience.

3. Cultivate Resilience:

- Resilience is the ability to bounce back from setbacks and adversity. Develop resilience by viewing challenges as opportunities for growth and learning.

- Practice resilience-building exercises, such as maintaining a gratitude journal and reframing negative thoughts.

4. Continuous Learning:

- Commit to lifelong learning. Whether it's through formal education, online courses, or self-study, expanding your knowledge and skills fosters personal growth.

- Read books, attend seminars, and seek out mentors who can facilitate your learning journey.

5. Practice Self-Compassion:

- Treat yourself with the same kindness and compassion that you would offer to a friend. Self-compassion is a powerful tool for personal growth and emotional well-being.

6. Step Outside Your Comfort Zone:

- Personal growth often occurs when you challenge yourself and step outside your comfort zone. Take calculated risks and embrace new experiences.

7. Build Healthy Habits:

- Healthy habits, such as regular exercise, balanced nutrition, and adequate sleep, are essential for personal growth. They support physical and mental well-being.

8. Reflect and Assess:

- Periodically assess your progress on your personal growth journey. Reflect on your accomplishments and areas where you can continue to improve.

9. Seek Inspiration:

- Surround yourself with inspirational figures, books, and content that motivate and empower you to grow. Seek out role models who embody the qualities you admire.

10. Practice Gratitude: - Cultivate a habit of gratitude by regularly acknowledging and appreciating the positive aspects of your life. Gratitude fosters a positive outlook and personal growth.

11. Establish Boundaries: - Setting healthy boundaries is crucial for personal growth and well-being. Learn to say no to commitments and situations that do not align with your values or deplete your energy.

12. Give Back: - Contributing to others through acts of kindness and volunteering can be a powerful source of personal growth and fulfillment.

Conclusion: The Endless Journey of Self-Discovery and Personal Growth

The journey of self-discovery and personal growth is a lifelong pursuit—a continuous evolution of your true self. It is a journey filled with self-awareness, resilience, and the unwavering commitment to living a life aligned with your values and aspirations.

As you embark on this transformative journey, remember that personal growth is not linear, and setbacks are a natural part of the process. Embrace each experience as an opportunity for learning and growth. Be patient and compassionate with yourself, for it is in the journey itself that you find the most profound discoveries and personal growth.

Ultimately, the path of self-discovery and personal growth leads to a life of authenticity, fulfillment, and purpose. It is a journey well worth embarking upon, as it empowers you to unlock your true potential and live a life that reflects the best of who you are.

The Future of Sigma Males: Navigating the Changing Landscape

The concept of Sigma males, with their unique blend of independence, self-reliance, and nonconformity, has captivated the imaginations of many. As society continues to evolve, the role of Sigma males in modern life is also undergoing transformation. In this exploration, we will delve into the future of Sigma males, speculating on their evolving role in contemporary society and discussing potential changes and trends that may shape their path forward.

The Shifting Social Landscape

To understand the future of Sigma males, it's essential to consider the broader social context in which they exist. Several key societal shifts are likely to impact the role of Sigma males in the years to come:

1. Technological Advancements:

- The rapid advancement of technology is reshaping the way we live and work. Automation, artificial intelligence, and remote work opportunities may provide Sigma males with more options for pursuing careers that align with their values and independence.

2. Changing Work Dynamics:

- Traditional workplace structures are evolving, with a greater emphasis on flexibility and freelancing. This shift could empower Sigma males to navigate their careers on their terms, engaging in project-based work or entrepreneurial ventures.

3. Emphasis on Mental Health:

- Society's growing recognition of mental health issues and the importance of self-care may encourage Sigma males to prioritize their emotional well-being and seek support when needed.

4. Expanding Awareness of Personality Types:

- As awareness of personality types and the diversity of human traits increases, Sigma males may find greater acceptance and understanding in society.

The Evolving Role of Sigma Males

With these societal shifts in mind, let's explore the potential changes and trends that could define the future of Sigma males:

1. Greater Embrace of Authenticity:

- As societal pressures to conform lessen, more individuals may embrace authenticity and nonconformity, leading to a broader acceptance of Sigma males and their values.

2. Entrepreneurship and Innovation:

- Sigma males' independent and innovative spirit may lead to a surge in entrepreneurial endeavors. Their ability to think outside the box and challenge the status quo could result in groundbreaking innovations and startups.

3. Work-Life Integration:

- The distinction between work and personal life is blurring. Sigma males may lead the way in developing work-life integration strategies that prioritize personal growth, well-being, and meaningful work.

4. Advocacy for Mental Health:

- Sigma males, who often value introspection and self-awareness, may play a role in advocating for mental health awareness and support within their communities and workplaces.

5. Influence in Thought Leadership:

- Sigma males' ability to think critically and independently could position them as thought leaders and influencers in various fields, sharing their insights and perspectives through media, literature, and public discourse.

6. Education and Mentorship:

- Sigma males may take on mentorship roles, guiding others in their journey of self-discovery, personal growth, and embracing authenticity.

7. Resilience and Adaptability:

- Their capacity for resilience and adaptability may serve Sigma males well in navigating the uncertainties and challenges of the future.

8. Relationship Dynamics:

- Sigma males may continue to seek and nurture relationships that align with their values of independence and authenticity. They may form connections with like-minded individuals who share their outlook on life.

Challenges and Considerations

While the future holds promise for Sigma males, it's essential to acknowledge potential challenges and considerations:

1. Balance and Well-Being:

- Maintaining a balance between independence and healthy social connections is crucial for overall well-being. Sigma males should be mindful of isolation and prioritize relationships that bring joy and fulfillment.

2. Adaptation to Change:

- As the world continues to change, Sigma males may need to adapt their approaches and strategies to thrive in evolving environments.

3. Navigating Traditional Expectations:

- Society's traditional expectations and norms may still persist in various contexts. Sigma males may encounter challenges when these expectations clash with their values and desires.

4. Self-Care and Mental Health:

- While self-reliance is a strength, it's essential for Sigma males to prioritize self-care and seek support when facing mental health challenges or emotional difficulties.

Conclusion: Embracing the Evolving Journey

The future of Sigma males is marked by both opportunities and challenges. As society undergoes profound transformations, Sigma males have the potential to play a significant role in shaping the world around them. Their values of authenticity, independence, and nonconformity align with the changing landscape, making them well-suited to embrace the evolving journey ahead.

For Sigma males, and indeed for all individuals, the key to thriving in this ever-changing world lies in embracing self-discovery, fostering personal growth, and staying true to one's authentic self. As they continue to navigate the shifting tides of modern society, Sigma males can inspire others to do the same—forging a path that celebrates individuality, innovation, and the unwavering commitment to living a life that reflects the best of who they are.

The Sigma Male's Guide to Leadership and Influence: Navigating the Path Less Traveled

Leadership and influence are not reserved solely for the charismatic Alphas or the conforming Betas. Sigma males, with their distinctive blend of independence, self-reliance, and nonconformity, possess a unique set of qualities that can make them highly effective leaders and influencers in various spheres of life. In this comprehensive guide, we will explore how Sigma males can harness their unique qualities to navigate the path less traveled and become impactful leaders and influencers.

Understanding Sigma Male Leadership

Before we delve into the strategies and techniques that Sigma males can use to excel as leaders and influencers, let's first understand the essence of Sigma male leadership:

1. Independence and Autonomy:

- Sigma males thrive on independence and autonomy. They are self-reliant and unafraid to take initiative, making them natural leaders who don't rely on external validation or authority.

2. Authenticity and Nonconformity:

- Sigma males prioritize authenticity over conformity. Their willingness to challenge norms and be their true selves sets them apart and attracts followers who resonate with their values.

3. Resilience and Adaptability:

- Sigma males' ability to navigate change and adversity with resilience and adaptability is a critical leadership trait. They don't shy away from challenges but see them as opportunities for growth.

4. Effective Communication:

- Effective communication is essential for any leader. Sigma males' straightforward and direct communication style can be a valuable asset in conveying their vision and ideas.

5. Empathy and Connection:

- Despite their independent nature, Sigma males often possess a deep sense of empathy and connection with others. This genuine care for individuals and causes can foster trust and followership.

Strategies for Sigma Male Leadership and Influence

Now, let's explore strategies and techniques that Sigma males can employ to become effective leaders and influencers:

1. Define Your Vision and Values:

- Effective leadership begins with a clear vision and a strong set of values. Define what you stand for and the impact you want to make in your chosen sphere.

2. Lead by Example:

- Sigma males are known for their authenticity. Lead by example, embodying the values and behaviors you want others to follow.

3. Cultivate Self-Awareness:

- Self-awareness is the foundation of effective leadership. Understand your strengths, weaknesses, and how your actions impact others.

4. Build Strong Relationships:

- While Sigma males value independence, strong relationships are essential for leadership. Cultivate genuine connections with your team or followers. Show empathy, listen actively, and be present.

5. Communicate Clearly and Directly:

- Sigma males' straightforward communication style can be an asset. Be clear and direct in your communication, conveying your ideas and expectations effectively.

6. Embrace Adaptability:

- In a rapidly changing world, adaptability is key. Embrace change and be open to new ideas and perspectives. Adjust your strategies when necessary without compromising your values.

7. Lead with Humility:

- Humility is a powerful leadership trait. Acknowledge your limitations, learn from mistakes, and be open to feedback.

8. Empower Others:

- Effective leaders empower others to reach their full potential. Provide opportunities for growth and development within your team or community.

9. Stay Committed to Self-Improvement:

- Sigma males value personal growth. Continuously invest in your own development, whether through education, self-improvement books, or mentorship.

10. Take Calculated Risks: - Don't be afraid to take calculated risks when opportunities arise. Sigma males' independence often allows them to see possibilities that others may overlook.

11. Advocate for Causes You Believe In: - Use your influence to advocate for causes and issues that align with your values. Sigma male leaders often have a strong sense of justice and fairness.

12. Embrace Authenticity in Leadership: - Authenticity is a cornerstone of Sigma male leadership. Be true to yourself and your values, even if it means going against the grain.

Challenges and Considerations

While Sigma males possess unique qualities that can make them effective leaders and influencers, there are challenges and considerations to keep in mind:

1. Building Trust: Sigma males may initially face challenges in building trust due to their independent nature. Consistency, authenticity, and empathy are essential to overcome this hurdle.

2. Balancing Independence and Collaboration: Finding the right balance between independence and collaboration is key. Effective leadership often involves working with others while maintaining your autonomy.

3. Managing Conflict: Sigma males may encounter conflict when their nonconformity clashes with traditional norms or established authority. Developing conflict resolution skills is crucial.

4. *Avoiding Isolation:* While independence is a strength, excessive isolation can hinder effective leadership. Cultivate a support network and seek feedback from trusted individuals.

Conclusion: Forging a Unique Path to Leadership and Influence

The future of leadership and influence in a rapidly changing world is not limited to a single archetype. Sigma males, with their distinctive qualities, have a unique role to play in shaping the future. By embracing their independence, authenticity, and resilience, Sigma males can lead and influence in a way that is true to their values and resonates with others who share their vision.

As Sigma males continue to navigate the path less traveled, they can inspire others to embrace their authentic selves, challenge the status quo, and make a meaningful impact in various spheres of life. The future of Sigma male leadership and influence is one of authenticity, innovation, and a commitment to forging a unique path to success.

Navigating the Sigma Male Lifestyle: Challenges and Rewards

The Sigma male lifestyle, characterized by independence, self-reliance, and nonconformity, offers a unique path to personal fulfillment and authenticity. However, like any way of life, it comes with its own set of challenges and rewards. In this exploration, we will delve into the day-to-day experiences of Sigma males, shedding light on the obstacles they may encounter and the rich rewards of living authentically and true to themselves.

Understanding the Sigma Male Lifestyle

Before we delve into the challenges and rewards, let's take a moment to understand what the Sigma male lifestyle entails:

1. Independence and Autonomy:

- Sigma males value their independence and autonomy above all else. They prefer making decisions for themselves and charting their own course in life.

2. Nonconformity and Authenticity:

- Authenticity is a core principle for Sigma males. They refuse to conform to societal norms or expectations that do not align with their values and beliefs.

3. Self-Reliance and Resilience:

- Sigma males possess a high degree of self-reliance and resilience. They are often self-sufficient and capable of navigating life's challenges independently.

4. Selective Social Connections:

- Sigma males tend to have a smaller, close-knit circle of friends and associates. They prioritize meaningful relationships over superficial ones.

5. Pursuit of Personal Growth:

- Personal growth and self-improvement are integral to the Sigma male lifestyle. They are driven by a desire to constantly learn and evolve.

Challenges of the Sigma Male Lifestyle

Now, let's explore the challenges that Sigma males may encounter in their day-to-day lives:

1. Social Isolation:

- Sigma males' preference for independence and selectivity in social connections can sometimes lead to feelings of isolation. They may struggle to relate to individuals who prioritize conformity and traditional social structures.

2. Misunderstanding and Stereotyping:

- Society often has preconceived notions about what it means to be a "real man" or a successful individual. Sigma males may face misunderstanding and stereotyping from those who don't comprehend their lifestyle choices.

3. Relationship Dynamics:

- Forming and maintaining romantic relationships can be challenging for Sigma males. Their desire for independence and authenticity may conflict with traditional relationship expectations.

4. Workplace Dynamics:

- In the workplace, Sigma males may face challenges related to conformity and hierarchical structures. They may find it difficult to fit into corporate environments that prioritize groupthink and conformity.

5. Resistance to Change:

- Sigma males' resistance to change can sometimes hinder their adaptability. In rapidly evolving industries or situations, they may struggle to adjust their perspectives or strategies.

6. Loneliness vs. Solitude:

- While solitude can be rejuvenating for Sigma males, it's essential to differentiate between solitude and loneliness. Loneliness can lead to emotional distress if not managed effectively.

7. Finding Meaningful Connections:

- Sigma males may struggle to find like-minded individuals who share their values and lifestyle. Building a supportive network of friends and allies can be a long and challenging process.

Rewards of the Sigma Male Lifestyle

Despite the challenges, the Sigma male lifestyle offers rich and meaningful rewards:

1. Authenticity and Fulfillment:

- Living authentically and true to oneself is a deeply rewarding experience. Sigma males derive a profound sense of fulfillment from pursuing their values and passions.

2. Personal Growth and Independence:

- The pursuit of personal growth and independence leads to continuous self-improvement. Sigma males relish the opportunity to develop their skills and knowledge.

3. Resilience and Self-Reliance:

- Sigma males' resilience and self-reliance empower them to face life's challenges head-on. They often emerge stronger and more capable after overcoming obstacles.

4. Meaningful Relationships:

- While Sigma males may have a smaller social circle, their relationships tend to be deeply meaningful and based on mutual respect and understanding.

5. Creativity and Innovation:

- Nonconformity and independent thinking often lead to creativity and innovation. Sigma males have the freedom to explore unconventional ideas and solutions.

6. Inner Peace and Solitude:

- Solitude is a source of inner peace and self-reflection for Sigma males. It provides a sanctuary for contemplation and personal growth.

7. Legacy of Authenticity:

- Sigma males often leave a lasting legacy of authenticity and nonconformity. They inspire others to be true to themselves and pursue their unique paths.

Navigating the Sigma Male Lifestyle: A Journey of Self-Discovery

The Sigma male lifestyle is not for everyone, but for those who choose it, it is a journey of self-discovery and personal growth. It challenges societal norms and expectations, offering a unique perspective on life and authenticity.

As Sigma males navigate the challenges and embrace the rewards of their lifestyle, they embody the values of independence, self-reliance, and nonconformity. They inspire others to consider their own paths, fostering a world where individuals are empowered to live authentically and true to themselves.

Sigma Males and Society's Expectations: Breaking Stereotypes

In a world where societal norms and expectations often shape our perceptions of masculinity and success, Sigma males stand apart as nonconformists. Their independent, self-reliant, and nontraditional approach to life challenges the stereotypes that society often places on individuals. In this exploration, we will examine the common stereotypes and societal expectations imposed on Sigma males and discuss strategies for breaking free from these constraints.

Unpacking the Sigma Male Stereotypes

Before we delve into strategies for breaking stereotypes, let's first understand the prevalent stereotypes that society often places on Sigma males:

1. Introversion Equals Weakness:

- One common stereotype is that Sigma males are introverted, and introversion is equated with weakness or social ineptitude. Society sometimes perceives introverts as lacking social skills or ambition.

2. Nonconformity as Rebellion:

- Nonconformity is often misinterpreted as rebellion or a refusal to cooperate. Sigma males' reluctance to conform to traditional norms and expectations may lead to misconceptions about their intentions.

3. Lone Wolf Mentality:

- The "lone wolf" stereotype suggests that Sigma males prefer isolation and are incapable of forming meaningful connections. This perception may lead to misunderstandings about their capacity for healthy relationships.

4. Career Independence as Unemployment:

- Sigma males' pursuit of career independence is sometimes viewed as unemployment or a lack of ambition. Society may question their ability to succeed in traditional career paths.

5. Emotional Stoicism:

- The stereotype of emotional stoicism suggests that Sigma males lack emotional depth or are incapable of expressing vulnerability. This can hinder authentic emotional connections.

6. Resistance to Authority:

- Sigma males' reluctance to conform to authority can be perceived as defiance or disrespect. This stereotype may hinder their ability to collaborate in professional settings.

Strategies for Breaking Stereotypes

Now, let's explore strategies for Sigma males to break free from these stereotypes and pave the way for a more authentic and fulfilling life:

1. Embrace Your Authentic Self:

- The first step in breaking stereotypes is to embrace your authentic self unapologetically. Recognize that your introversion, nonconformity, and independence are strengths, not weaknesses.

2. Educate and Communicate:

- Educate those around you about Sigma male traits and values. Open, honest communication can dispel misconceptions and foster understanding.

3. Foster Meaningful Relationships:

- While Sigma males value independence, meaningful relationships are essential for personal growth and support. Prioritize relationships that align with your values.

4. Showcase Your Strengths:

- Demonstrate your strengths, whether in the workplace or in your personal life. Let your achievements and capabilities speak for themselves.

5. Seek Mentorship:

- Find mentors or role models who have successfully navigated similar challenges. Their guidance can be invaluable in shaping your own path.

6. Challenge Stereotypes Through Actions:

- Challenge stereotypes by taking actions that defy expectations. Show that nonconformity can lead to innovation and success.

7. Embrace Emotional Intelligence:

- While emotional stoicism is a stereotype, emotional intelligence is a powerful tool. Develop your emotional awareness and communication skills to build more profound connections.

8. Collaborate on Your Terms:

- In professional settings, collaborate on your terms. Be clear about your expectations and boundaries while still respecting the needs of the team.

9. Be Resilient in the Face of Resistance:

- Recognize that resistance to nonconformity is natural. Be resilient in the face of criticism or pushback, and stay true to your values and principles.

10. Advocate for Authenticity: - Advocate for authenticity in society. Encourage others to embrace their unique qualities and challenge stereotypes.

11. Share Your Journey: - Consider sharing your personal journey and experiences as a Sigma male. Your story can inspire others to break free from societal expectations.

12. Find Supportive Communities: - Seek out communities and networks of like-minded individuals who understand and appreciate your perspective. These connections can provide a sense of belonging.

Conclusion: Redefining Success on Your Terms

Breaking stereotypes is a continuous journey that requires determination and resilience. Sigma males, by embracing their authenticity and challenging societal expectations, have the power to redefine success on their terms. They can inspire others to do the same, fostering a world where individuals are free to be true to themselves, pursue their passions, and live a life that aligns with their values.

As Sigma males navigate their unique paths, they demonstrate that authenticity, independence, and nonconformity are not weaknesses but strengths that can lead to a life of fulfillment and purpose. In doing so, they contribute to a more inclusive and diverse society that celebrates individuality and empowers everyone to break free from limiting stereotypes.

Sigma Male Archetypes in Pop Culture: Unmasking the Nonconformists

In the vast tapestry of popular culture, certain characters and figures have emerged as exemplars of the Sigma male archetype. These individuals, whether in film, literature, or other forms of media, embody the traits of independence, self-reliance, and nonconformity that define Sigma males. In this exploration, we will analyze the Sigma male archetypes in pop culture, dissecting their portrayal and examining their impact on our perceptions of nonconformist masculinity.

Defining the Sigma Male Archetype

Before we delve into the characters, it's important to clarify what defines the Sigma male archetype:

1. Independence and Autonomy:

- Sigma males prioritize independence and autonomy, often pursuing their goals and passions on their terms without seeking external validation.

2. Nonconformity and Authenticity:

- Authenticity is at the core of Sigma male identity. They refuse to conform to societal norms or expectations that do not align with their values and beliefs.

3. Self-Reliance and Resilience:

- Sigma males possess a high degree of self-reliance and resilience. They are often self-sufficient and capable of navigating life's challenges independently.

4. Selective Social Connections:

- Sigma males tend to have a smaller, close-knit circle of friends and associates. They prioritize meaningful relationships over superficial ones.

5. Pursuit of Personal Growth:

- Personal growth and self-improvement are integral to the Sigma male lifestyle. They are driven by a desire to constantly learn and evolve.

Sigma Male Archetypes in Pop Culture

Now, let's examine some iconic characters and figures in pop culture who embody the Sigma male archetype and explore their portrayal and impact:

**1. *James Bond (007):*

- James Bond, the suave and enigmatic British spy, epitomizes the Sigma male. He is fiercely independent, values self-reliance, and is known for his nonconformist approach to espionage.

2. *Tyler Durden (Fight Club):*

- Tyler Durden from "Fight Club" represents the dark, rebellious side of the Sigma male. He rejects consumerism and societal norms, advocating for personal liberation through chaos.

3. *John Wick (John Wick franchise):*

- John Wick is a legendary assassin who lives by his own code. His relentless pursuit of justice and revenge showcases the resilience and self-reliance of a Sigma male.

4. *Han Solo (Star Wars):*

- Han Solo, the charming rogue from the "Star Wars" universe, embodies the Sigma male traits of independence and nonconformity. His journey from smuggler to hero showcases personal growth.

5. *Rorschach (Watchmen):*

- Rorschach, from the graphic novel "Watchmen," is an uncompromising vigilante who adheres to his strict moral code. His unwavering commitment to justice illustrates the resilience of a Sigma male.

6. Wolverine (X-Men):

- Wolverine, also known as Logan, is a brooding antihero who operates by his own rules. His solitary nature and resilience in the face of adversity reflect Sigma male qualities.

7. Rick Grimes (The Walking Dead):

- Rick Grimes, the leader in "The Walking Dead" series, showcases the Sigma male's journey from reluctant leader to a resilient protector of his group.

8. Jason Bourne (Bourne franchise):

- Jason Bourne is a skilled operative who navigates a complex web of espionage. His independence, adaptability, and pursuit of truth align with Sigma male traits.

9. V (V for Vendetta):

- V, the enigmatic protagonist of "V for Vendetta," embodies nonconformity and resistance against oppressive systems, exemplifying the Sigma male's quest for personal freedom.

10. Sherlock Holmes (Sherlock Holmes stories): - Sherlock Holmes, the brilliant detective, values intellectual independence and nonconformity. His pursuit of truth and justice align with Sigma male principles.

Impact and Influence

The portrayal of Sigma male archetypes in pop culture has had a profound impact on our understanding of nonconformist masculinity. These characters and figures challenge traditional stereotypes of heroism and redefine what it means to be a strong, independent individual. Their stories resonate with audiences because they reflect the universal desire for personal freedom, authenticity, and resilience.

Conclusion: Sigma Male Archetypes as Catalysts for Change

The Sigma male archetypes in pop culture serve as catalysts for change, inspiring individuals to question societal norms and embrace their authentic selves. Through their portrayal, these characters and figures challenge us to reevaluate our perceptions of masculinity and success, encouraging us to prioritize independence, self-reliance, and personal growth.

As we continue to encounter Sigma male archetypes in various forms of media, we are reminded that the path of the nonconformist is not one of isolation but of empowerment and authenticity. These characters demonstrate that it is possible to break free from societal expectations, pursue our passions, and live life on our own terms—a message that resonates deeply with those who aspire to embrace the Sigma male lifestyle in their own unique ways.

Sigma Males and Personal Fulfillment: Finding Your Path

Personal fulfillment is a universal pursuit, but for Sigma males, it often takes a unique form. Defined by their independence, self-reliance, and nonconformity, Sigma males seek a path that aligns with their values and principles. In this exploration, we will provide guidance on how Sigma males can navigate their journey towards personal fulfillment, offering strategies to help them find their path and achieve a deep sense of purpose and contentment.

The Quest for Personal Fulfillment

Before we delve into guidance for Sigma males, it's important to understand the concept of personal fulfillment and why it holds particular significance for individuals who identify with the Sigma male archetype:

1. Defining Personal Fulfillment:

- Personal fulfillment is the sense of satisfaction, contentment, and purpose that arises when individuals align their actions, choices, and pursuits with their core values and beliefs.

2. Embracing Individuality:

- For Sigma males, personal fulfillment often involves embracing their individuality, pursuing their passions, and living life on their terms, free from societal pressures to conform.

3. Nonconformity and Authenticity:

- Authenticity is a core principle for Sigma males. Achieving personal fulfillment means staying true to oneself, even in the face of societal expectations to conform.

4. Personal Growth and Self-Improvement:

- Sigma males are driven by a desire for personal growth and self-improvement. This journey of continuous learning and development is integral to their sense of fulfillment.

Guidance for Sigma Males on the Path to Personal Fulfillment

Now, let's explore strategies and guidance for Sigma males to find their path to personal fulfillment:

1. Clarify Your Values:

- Begin by clarifying your core values and beliefs. What matters most to you? What principles guide your life? Understanding your values is the first step toward aligning your actions with them.

2. Define Your Own Success:

- Challenge societal definitions of success. Define success on your terms, considering what truly fulfills you rather than external markers of achievement.

3. Embrace Independence:

- Embrace your independence and self-reliance. Understand that it's okay to pursue your goals and passions without seeking external validation or approval.

4. Pursue Your Passions:

- Identify your passions and interests, and make them a central part of your life. Engaging in activities you love can bring a profound sense of fulfillment.

5. Prioritize Personal Growth:

- Commit to continuous personal growth and self-improvement. Whether through education, skill development, or self-reflection, prioritize your journey of self-betterment.

6. Seek Authentic Connections:

- While Sigma males value independence, meaningful relationships are still crucial for personal fulfillment. Cultivate authentic connections with individuals who respect your autonomy and values.

7. Balance Solitude and Social Engagement:

- Balance your need for solitude and self-reflection with social engagement. Solitude can be rejuvenating, but meaningful connections with others also contribute to personal fulfillment.

8. Set Meaningful Goals:

- Set goals that resonate with your values and passions. These goals will serve as a roadmap for your journey toward personal fulfillment.

9. Embrace Adaptability:

- Be open to change and adaptability. The path to personal fulfillment may involve evolving strategies and goals as you grow and learn.

10. Practice Mindfulness: - Mindfulness and self-awareness are essential for personal fulfillment. Regularly check in with yourself to ensure that your actions align with your values and bring you happiness.

11. Give Back and Contribute: - Contributing to causes or communities you care about can enhance your sense of fulfillment. Sigma males can make a meaningful impact by channeling their independence and strengths toward causes they believe in.

12. Celebrate Your Authenticity: - Celebrate your authenticity and nonconformity. Recognize that your unique qualities are strengths that set you apart and contribute to your personal fulfillment.

Challenges and Considerations

While personal fulfillment is a worthy pursuit, it's important to acknowledge potential challenges and considerations for Sigma males:

1. Balance Independence and Collaboration:

- Finding the right balance between independence and collaboration in both personal and professional life can be challenging.

2. Navigating Societal Expectations:

- Sigma males may encounter resistance or misunderstanding from those who expect conformity. Learning to navigate societal expectations is an ongoing process.

3. Self-Care and Mental Health:

- Prioritize self-care and mental health. Personal fulfillment is closely tied to well-being, so it's essential to seek support when needed.

4. Embracing Change:

- Be adaptable and willing to embrace change, as personal fulfillment often involves growth and transformation.

Conclusion: Forging a Fulfilling and Purposeful Path

Personal fulfillment for Sigma males is not a one-size-fits-all journey but a deeply personal and individual path. It involves aligning one's actions with core values, pursuing passions, and embracing authenticity. The Sigma male's commitment to personal growth and self-improvement fuels this journey, leading to a life of purpose and contentment.

As Sigma males navigate their unique paths toward personal fulfillment, they inspire others to do the same, demonstrating that authenticity, independence, and nonconformity are not obstacles but powerful tools for finding meaning and purpose in a world that often expects conformity. The quest for personal fulfillment is a lifelong journey, and Sigma males serve as beacons of empowerment, showing us that it is possible to live a life that reflects the best of who we are.

Conclusion: Embracing the Sigma Male Lifestyle

In the journey we've undertaken throughout this book, we've explored the intriguing world of Sigma males—the individuals who defy conventional norms, prioritize independence, and embody nonconformity. We've delved deep into their distinctive qualities, lifestyle, challenges, and rewards. Now, as we draw this book to a close, it's time to summarize the key takeaways and encourage you, the reader, to apply the valuable insights you've gained to your own life.

Key Takeaways from the Book

1. **Sigma Males Are Unique Individuals:**

    - Sigma males are a unique breed. They prioritize independence, self-reliance, and authenticity, often challenging societal expectations and norms.

2. **Embrace Your Authenticity:**

    - Authenticity is at the core of the Sigma male lifestyle. Embrace your true self, values, and beliefs, even if they diverge from societal expectations.

3. **Nonconformity as Strength:**

- Nonconformity is not a weakness but a strength. Sigma males demonstrate that it's possible to chart your own path and succeed on your terms.

4. *Independence and Self-Reliance Matter:*

    - Independence and self-reliance are central to the Sigma male lifestyle. These qualities empower you to make decisions based on your own judgment and values.

5. *Personal Growth Is a Lifelong Journey:*

    - Personal growth and self-improvement are integral to Sigma males. The pursuit of knowledge, skills, and self-awareness is a lifelong journey.

6. *Balance Solitude and Connection:*

    - Finding a balance between solitude for self-reflection and meaningful connections with others is crucial for a fulfilling life.

7. *Challenge Stereotypes and Expectations:*

    - Sigma males often face stereotypes and societal expectations. Challenge these preconceptions and strive to redefine success on your terms.

8. **Lead and Influence Authentically:**

    - Sigma males have the potential to be effective leaders and influencers. Lead with authenticity, humility, and a commitment to your values.

9. **Navigate Challenges Resiliently:**

    - Life brings challenges, but Sigma males navigate them with resilience and adaptability. Embrace change and learn from adversity.

10. **Embrace Personal Fulfillment:**

    - Personal fulfillment is the ultimate goal. Define success on your own terms, prioritize your passions, and embrace a life that aligns with your values.

Applying What You've Learned

As you've journeyed through the pages of this book, you've gained insights into the Sigma male lifestyle and philosophy. Now, it's time to apply these lessons to your own life:

1. Embrace Your Authenticity:

- Take a moment to reflect on your values and beliefs. Embrace your authentic self and don't be afraid to express your uniqueness.

2. Pursue Personal Growth:

- Commit to a journey of personal growth and self-improvement. Identify areas where you can learn and develop, and take action to expand your knowledge and skills.

3. Find Your Balance:

- Strive to find a balance between solitude for self-reflection and meaningful connections with others. Cultivate relationships that support and uplift you.

4. Challenge Stereotypes:

- Be aware of stereotypes and societal expectations that may limit your potential. Challenge these preconceptions and define success on your terms.

5. Lead with Authenticity:

- Whether in your personal or professional life, lead with authenticity. Embrace your unique leadership style and values.

6. Navigate Challenges Resiliently:

- Approach challenges with resilience and adaptability. Embrace change as an opportunity for growth and learning.

7. Prioritize Personal Fulfillment:

- Above all, prioritize personal fulfillment. Define what it means to you, set meaningful goals, and take action to align your life with your values and passions.

Continuing the Journey

The journey of a Sigma male is one of self-discovery, growth, and authenticity. It's a journey that acknowledges the strength in nonconformity, the power of individuality, and the fulfillment found in living life on your terms.

As you continue your journey, remember that you are not alone. Others who resonate with the Sigma male lifestyle are walking alongside you, each forging their unique path. Together, you can challenge the status quo, redefine success, and inspire others to embrace their authentic selves.

In a world that often prioritizes conformity, your unique perspective is a beacon of empowerment. Your choices, actions, and values have the power to shape not only your own life but also the lives of those around you. You have the capacity to inspire change, foster authenticity, and contribute to a world where individuality is celebrated.

So, embrace the Sigma male lifestyle, not as a rigid identity, but as a philosophy that guides you toward a life of purpose, contentment, and fulfillment. Continue your journey with courage, curiosity, and the unwavering belief that you have the power to live life on your own terms—a life that is true to yourself.

Made in the USA
Columbia, SC
27 December 2024